D0844538

BOOK SOLD
NO LONGER R.H.P.L.
PROPERTY

RICHMOND HILL
PUBLIC LIBRARY
DEC 23 2015
RICHVALE
905-889-2847

RN

Carey Price

by Jennifer Sutoski

CAPSTONE PRESS
a capstone imprint

Pebble Plus is published by Capstone Press,
1710 Roe Crest Drive, North Mankato, Minnesota 56003
www.capstonepub.com

Copyright © 2016 by Capstone Press, a Capstone imprint. All rights reserved. No part of this publication may be reproduced in whole or in part, or stored in a retrieval system, or transmitted in any form or by any means, electronic, mechanical, photocopying, recording, or otherwise, without written permission of the publisher.

Library of Congress Cataloging-in-Publication Data
Cataloging-in-publication information is on file with the Library of Congress.

ISBN 978–1-4914-7835-6 (library binding : alk. paper)
ISBN 978–1-4914-7843-1 (pbk. : alk. paper)
ISBN 978–1-4914-7858-5 (eBook PDF)

Developed and Produced by Discovery Books Limited
Paul Humphrey: project manager
Sabrina Crewe: editor
Ian Winton: designer

Photo Credits
Chris Szagola/AP/Corbis: cover, 13 (main image); Reuters/Brian Snyder/Corbis: title page, 19; Courtesy of Dylan Walsh, Nagwuntl'oo School, Ulkatcho First Nation: 5; Wikimedia Commons: 7 (main image); Richard Wolowicz/Getty Images: 7 (inset); Chris Relke/Getty Images: 9 (main image); Dean Bertoncelj/Shutterstock: 9 (inset); Anders Wiklund/EPA/Corbis: 11; Meunierd/Shutterstock: 13 (inset); Richard Wolowicz/Getty Images: 15; Christian Petersen/Getty Images: 17; Michael Wigle/www.mwigle.zenfolio.com: 21.

Note to Parents and Teachers
The Canadian Biographies set supports national curriculum standards for social studies related to people and culture. This book describes and illustrates Carey Price. The images support early readers in understanding text. The repetition of words and phrases helps early readers learn new words. This book also introduces early readers to subject-specific vocabulary words, which are defined in the Glossary section. Early readers may need assistance to read some words and to use the Table of Contents, Glossary, Read More, Internet Sites, and Index sections of the book.

Printed in China through World Print Ltd in 2015
007326WPF15

Table of Contents

Early Years

Carey Price was born August 16, 1987. Carey and his sister Kayla grew up in Anahim Lake, BC. Their mother Lynda was chief of the Ulkatcho First Nation. Carey learned to skate on a creek.

born in Vancouver

1987

A sign in Anahim Lake shows that people there are proud of Carey.

Carey started playing ice hockey as a goaltender in Williams Lake. It took more than six hours to drive there and back. So Carey's dad bought a plane to take his son to practice!

born in
Vancouver

1987

1997

starts
practising in
Williams Lake

Carey's father Jerry was a goaltender, too.

Carey went to play hockey in a little plane like this one.

Junior Hockey

Carey began playing junior hockey in 2003. He played for the Tri-City Americans. He did so well that the Montreal Canadiens picked him in the draft.

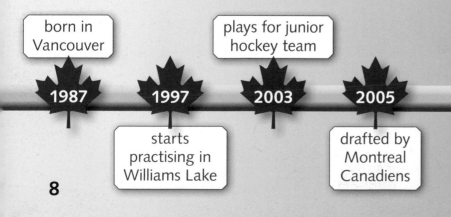

born in Vancouver

plays for junior hockey team

1987　1997　2003　2005

starts practising in Williams Lake

drafted by Montreal Canadiens

Carey's junior team was in the Western Hockey League (WHL).

The Montreal Canadiens are in the National Hockey League (NHL).

2007 was Carey's last year as a junior. He went with Team Canada to the World Junior Championships in Sweden. Team Canada won the championship. Carey was named Most Valuable Player.

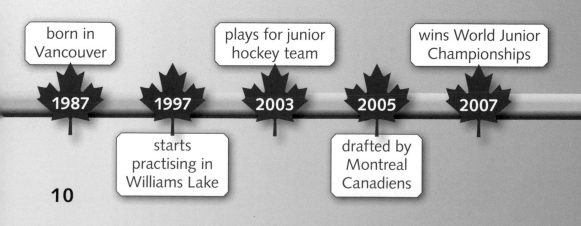

born in Vancouver

plays for junior hockey team

wins World Junior Championships

1987   1997   2003   2005   2007

starts practising in Williams Lake

drafted by Montreal Canadiens

10

Carey saves a shot at the 2007 World Junior Championships.

The Canadiens

Carey began playing for the
Canadiens. He became a star
in his first year. He won many
awards for his goaltending.
Carey had hard years, too.
His team lost some games.

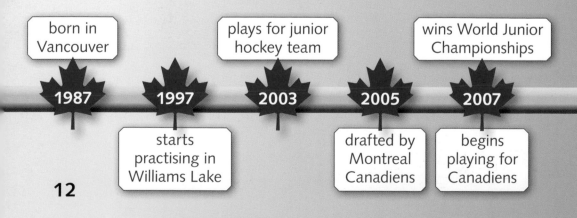

born in
Vancouver

plays for junior
hockey team

wins World Junior
Championships

1987   **1997**   **2003**   **2005**   **2007**

starts
practising in
Williams Lake

drafted by
Montreal
Canadiens

begins
playing for
Canadiens

On this sign, the Canadiens are called by their nickname, the "Habs."

Carey tosses the puck.

Carey is proud to be part of the
Ulkatcho First Nation. He helped
at the 2010 championships for
young Aboriginal athletes. In
2011, Carey won his 100th
game in the NHL.

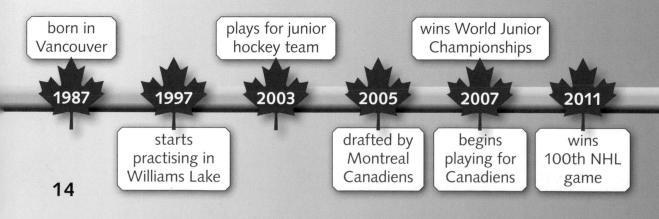

born in
Vancouver

plays for junior
hockey team

wins World Junior
Championships

1987   1997   2003   2005   2007   2011

starts
practising in
Williams Lake

drafted by
Montreal
Canadiens

begins
playing for
Canadiens

wins
100th NHL
game

Carey stops a puck in his 100th NHL game.

In 2012, the Canadiens signed up Carey for another six years. He kept playing and winning awards. Carey played in All-Star games, too. He married his girlfriend Angela in 2013.

born in Vancouver

1987

plays for junior hockey team

1997

starts practising in Williams Lake

2003

wins World Junior Championships

2005

drafted by Montreal Canadiens

2007

begins playing for Canadiens

2011

wins 100th NHL game

signs with Canadiens

2012

2013

marries Angela Webber

Carey signs an autograph at the 2012 NHL All-Star Game.

Winning Gold

Carey was on Canada's team at the 2014 Olympic Games in Russia. Canada won a gold medal. Carey made all 24 saves in the finals. He was named best goaltender at the Olympics.

born in Vancouver
1987

starts practising in Williams Lake
1997

plays for junior hockey team
2003

drafted by Montreal Canadiens
2005

wins World Junior Championships
2007

begins playing for Canadiens
2011

wins 100th NHL game
2012

signs with Canadiens
2013

marries Angela Webber
2014

wins Olympic gold medal

Carey and Canada's other goalies receive their Olympic gold medals.

Canadiens' coach Michel Therrien says, "Carey gives us confidence as a team every game." When he's not playing hockey, Carey likes to be outdoors. He enjoys calf roping and hunting.

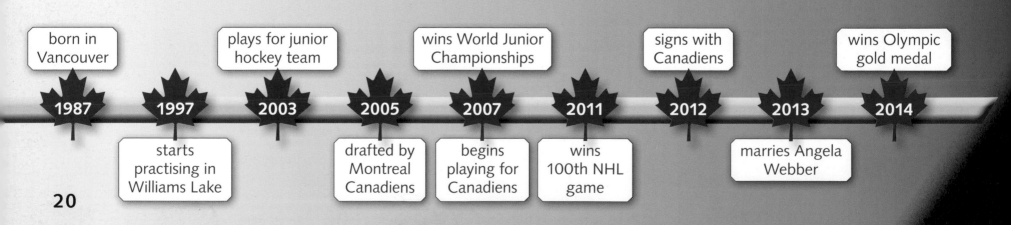

born in Vancouver
1987

starts practising in Williams Lake
1997

plays for junior hockey team
2003

drafted by Montreal Canadiens
2005

wins World Junior Championships
2007

begins playing for Canadiens
2011

wins 100th NHL game
2012

signs with Canadiens
2013

marries Angela Webber
2014

wins Olympic gold medal

Carey likes to rope calves in rodeos.

Glossary

award—something people get for winning or doing well

championships—the games or contests that decide who is the best of all

confidence—what a person has when they are sure they can do something well

creek—a stream of water smaller than a river

draft—a process of picking something

finals—the last game or contest that decides the winner

goaltender—the person who guards the goal in a game of hockey

Olympic Games—world event at which countries compete in many different sports

valuable—something very precious and important

Read More

Biskup, Agnieszka. *Ice Hockey: How It Works.* Chicago, IL: Raintree, 2012.

Doeden, Matt. *Carey Price.* New York: Sports Illustrated for Kids, 2015.

Internet Sites

FactHound offers a safe, fun way to find Internet sites related to this book. All of the sites on FactHound have been researched by our staff.

Here's all you do:

Visit *www.facthound.com*

Type in this code: 9781491478356

 Check out projects, games and lots more at
www.capstonekids.com

Index